a Enrico,
e a Marta, Matilde, Bianca

©2008 by HELVETIA EDITRICE

30038 SPINEA (VE)
via Pozzuoli 9
tel. 041-994550
fax 041-5086514
www.edizionihelvetia.it
info@edizionihelvetia.it

ISBN: 978-88-95215-11-2

Titolo originale: A spasso per Venezia
Traduzione di Jennifer James

Prima edizione: febbraio 2008

Finito di stampare
nel mese di febbraio 2008
presso Arcari srl
Mogliano Veneto (TV)

Stampato in Italia
Printed in Italy

Un grazie particolare
a Gabriella Fregonese
a Eleonora Scarpa
a Luisa Turchi

A WALK THROUGH VENICE
WITH MARTA JACOPO AND LULA

A MINIGUIDE
FOR THE BIG TRAVELLERS

written and illustrated by Maria Gianola

Hello!

I am Marta and this is my brother Jacopo

Would you like to come with us and

take tour of VENICE ?

2

Also Grandfather Bepi will come with us
to tell us very curious stories about Venice,
its birth, its traditions, its holidays,
its story, and the painters and the artists that beautified the city
with their works of art.

Then we will also listen to its magical stories:
stories of fear, stories of enchantment, stories of kings and queens,
of rare flowers and rings of gold.

GRANDFATHER BEPI.

LULA

...But where's Lula?
Lula! Come here!
We have to go,
VENICE is waiting for us!

Ready friends?
Let's go!

3

1 - HOW IS VENICE MADE?

Venice is the shape of a fish.

It rises above an archipelago of a hundred small islands of varied shapes and sizes and it is about 4 km (2.5 miles) from the mainland, to which it is connected by a bridge so that cars and trains may pass.

It is divided in 6 zones called sestieri (districts):
>   Castello, Cannaregio, San Marco,
>   San Polo, Santa Croce, Dorsoduro.

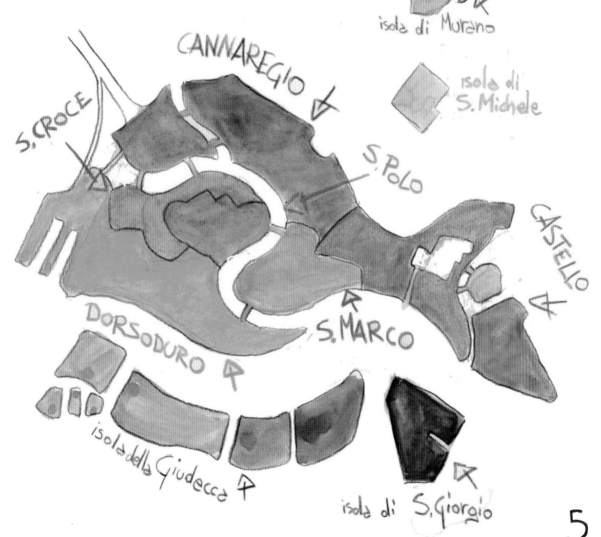

CANNAREGIO ↗

S.CROCE

S.POLO

CASTELLO ↗

DORSODURO ↗

S.MARCO ↗

isola di Murano ↗

isola di S. Michele

isola della Giudecca ↗

isola di S.Giorgio ↗

5

THE STRUCTURE AND FOUNDATION

The formation and the development of Venice happened slowly over the course of the centuries: its first inhabitants situated themselves around the islands that would later become the heart of Venice (Isole Realtine), seat of the doge (elected official), and the center of power and commerce. The swampy ground was drained by reinforcing the shorelines where the flowing water ran between island and island, and by planting long poles of wood in the ground to strengthen the foundation of the constructions and buildings to prevent them from sinking into the muddy layer.

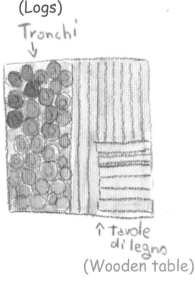

(Logs)
Tronchi ↓

↑ Tavole di legno
(Wooden table)

(Ground)
Suolo

Acqua (Water)

Fango (Mud)

Argilla (Clay)

6

The houses where then built above
solid slabs of larch (type of wood).

The poles hammered into the mud became
so resisting and cemented between them
that they preserved themselves for centuries
in excellent conditions, by not finding
themselves in contact with the air.

GRANDFATHER TOLD ME
THAT UNDER THE CHURCH
OF THE MADONNA DELLA SALUTE,
THERE ARE 1,150,657 TREE TRUNKS
PLANTED TO SUPPORT IT:
AN ENTIRE FOREST DESTROYED!

CALLI, CAMPI, CAMPIELLI

Come on, let us go learn some Venetian names!

A narrow road between two houses is called a calle,
but if is more spacious it is a calle larga.
The squares (piazze), instead call themselves campi (fields), because,
in the entire city, the only square is... which? Saint Mark Square!

In the middle to every campo (field), campiello (small field),
or corte (court) there is almost always a well-curb, once
used to drain rain water: the water entered in by the
four drains surrounding the well and was then filtered
by a layer of sand. They exist of every period and style;
some of them are true and actual works of art!

WELL-CURB FROM THE
THIRTEENTH CENTURY
BUILT IN RED MARBLE
IN CORTE DEL TENTOR

The roads that run long the canals
are called fondamente, excluded
those around the Grand Canal
which are called rive. Some roads
are rughe, a term stolen from the
French word "rue" which means road.
Others are called salizada which means
paved, a name given to the first calli
that had been paved with stones of
trachyte by Colli Euganei,
the well-known masonry.

8

...AND LOOK HERE ABOVE. THE WALL
OF THE FIRST FLOOR IS PROTRUDING;
RESTRICTING THE SPACE ABOVE
THE CALLE: IT IS SUPPORTED BY BRACKETS OF WOOD
THAT CAN SUSTAIN A CONSIDERABLE WEIGHT,
THUS CREATING A USEFUL SHELTER FOR THE SHOPS.

9

NIZIOLETI

The names of calli, campi, campielli, ponti (bridges)
are written on nizioleti, they are called this because
they look like small sheets.
The names are painted in black on a painted white
background in the shape of a rectangle: they are characteristic also
because they are written in dialect, names given to places from the
mangling of its original name by the Venetian people, for example,
the church San Gervasio and Protasio became with the years San Trovaso,
San Eustachio became in itself San Stae, San Ermagora and Fortunato
has transformed into San Marcuola!

·Also, the municipal numbers
are painted black on a small
white oval background,
emphasized with a black border.

A municipal number in Venice can
have also 4 numbers:
in every district the municipal
numbers begin from 1 and
continue progressively until
the end of the district.
The district of Castello
continues until the number 6828!

10

PONTE
STORTO

170

1029

WHEN WALKING IN VENICE, ONE NEEDS TO STOP EVERY SO OFTEN TO REFRESH AND QUENCH THEIR THIRST, LIKE FROM THIS **FOUNTAIN** WHICH POURS GOOD AND **FRESH WATER**! THERE IS ONE IN ALMOST EVERY CAMPO.

11

THE CANALS

As we have seen, Venice was born and was developed
in the water: while the houses, churches, and palaces
were built on these islands, the shorelines became
strengthened, giving origin to the paths of the
channels that flow throughout every corner of the city.
Already in the 6th century the Venetians moved
themselves by water and tied up their boats to
the walls of their houses (as was done with horses).
The houses that were built the closest to the water
positioned the main entrance towards the channel:
behind the houses, towards the inside of the island,
there were the backyards with cultivated gardens.

Also the churches were built with their entrances
facing the water. The canals were therefore, for
a long period of time, the main roads of transportation
and the life of Venice: today if you count them, there
are about 150 canals.
The water level in the numerous canals continually
changes because of high and low tides, which also
creates the phenomenon of the high water (see page 108);
for 6 hours the water level rises and is flushed in ad out
of the lagoon from the sea, and vice versa, across the
mouth of the port, also performing an important daily
cleansing of the city.

THE GRAND CANAL

The most important of the canals in Venice is the Grand Canal that curves twice to form the shape of the letter "S" and cuts the city into two parts (the Venetians often say "says citra" and "says ultra", to indicate on which side of the canal one can be found in respect to Saint Mark's Square).

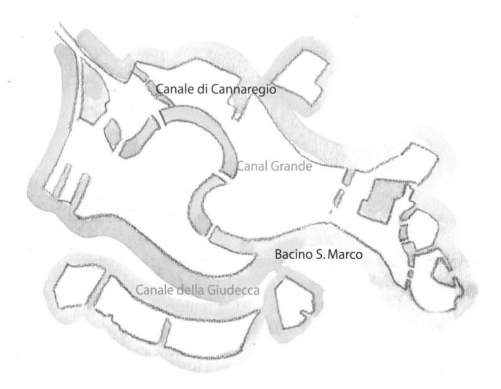

14

The Grand Canal is about 4 km long (2.5 miles), from Piazzale Roma (the parking garage) until Bacino San Marco.

It is crossed by 4 bridges: ponte di Rialto, ponte degli Scalzi, ponte dell'Accademia (in wood), and the new bridge made of glass and steel, designed by the Spanish architect Calatrava, that unites Piazzale Roma to the railway station.

It is possible to travel down the entire Grand Canal by vaporetto, a unique mode of public transportation only seen in Venice (see page 112): from which you can view both sides of the canals and its palaces of the richest and most noble Venetian families those of whom still carry their name until today: Ca' Dario, Ca' Foscari, Ca' da Mosto, ex...
The spikes on the roof of the palace indicated the presence of a "captain of the sea" of the Venetian fleet. Every noble family, in front of their palace, had a moored tied up to poles of wood that were painted of various colors with the family coat of arms.

15

THE BRIDGES

The 416 bridges that cross over the network of canals throughout the city are different in type, form and dimension: originally, all the bridges were built with wooden planks forming a flat slope to allow the passage of the carts and the horses.

They later decided to rebuild the bridges in stone and brick, to form an arc with steps. The railings were added in 1800, due to an increase in pedestrian use after the construction of the two new bridges on the Grand Canal (besides the Rialto Bridge): the Accademia Bridge, the Scalzi Bridge (to the train station). Until then, Venetians considered the canals the main source of transportation in the city.

The name of every bridge is written on the nizioleto (see page 10) and takes its name from: the place in which the bridge is found (ponte dell'Ospedaletto); its shape (crooked bridge – ponte Storto, bridge of three arcs – ponte dei Tre Archi), or the occupation more common in that place (bridge of the blacksmiths – ponte dei Fabbri, bridge of the bakers – ponte del Forner)

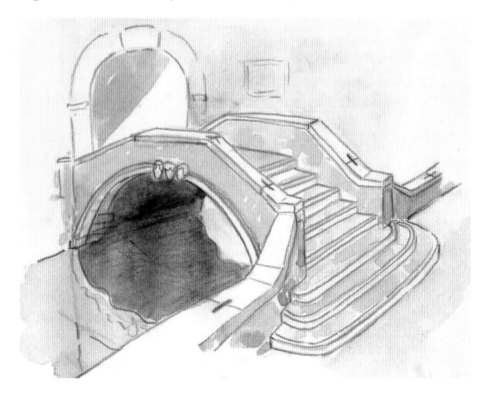

RIALTO BRIDGE

The Rialto Bridge was the first bridge made of stone
on the Grand Canal: in the 12th century it was a bridge
of boats united by planks of wood and was called the
Bridge of the Coin (ponte della Moneta), in memory of
the toll that one had to pay to the ferryman
when the bridge was not there.

It collapsed because of the overflowing crowd of people
admiring the procession of the Marquis of Ferrara.
In 1444, it was rebuilt again in wood, but wider and with
two rows of shops on either side of the bridge.
There was also a drawbridge station for the passage
of the sail boats.

THE RIALTO BRIDGE IN WOOD IS REPRESENTED
HERE IN THIS WELL-KNOWN PAINTING
BY VITTORE CARPACCIO.

18

In the 1500's the Senate decided to rebuild it in stone. For this occasion there were numerous designs presented by many architects, of these were that of Michelangelo and of Andrea Palladio: in the end however, the project was given to the engineer Antonio Da Ponte, who combined the ideas of the different proposals, which resulted in the splendid design that until today is still admired.

19

THE BRIDGE OF SIGHS

The Bridge of Sighs, which connects the Doge's Palace with the Palace of the Prisons, was used to transport prisoners from the jail to the magistrate where the trial took place.

It is an aerial bridge that was designed and built to ensure the greatest safety measures against every attempt of escape: it is situated on the first floor, closed on every side, and has only two small sun windows.

The prisoners crossed the bridge on their way to confront the trial, and perhaps their conviction. Tradition says, that when the prisoners looked out beyond the windows, they sighed at their last view of Venice and at the thought of their sad destiny.

BRIDGE OF THE DEVIL

Another very well-known bridge is the Bridge of the Devil. It is an authentic traditional bridge, because it entirely lacks railings, as were all bridges of Venice until the middle of the 1800's. It is found on the island of Torcello, in one of the more poetic and characteristic sites of the Lagoon.

In Venice, only one other bridge without railings can be found: Bridge of Nails (Ponte Chiodo), along the Fondamenta of S. Felice in the district of Cannaregio.

A story of Grandfather Bepi

The holiday of Saint Martin

Dear Children,
The story that I will tell you took place during the time of the ancient Romans.

The winter had just begun in the year 338, and one particular night it was extremely cold. In the white army, a young brave soldier on horseback served the Imperial Roman Guard. He wore traditional armour, and carried a shield, a sword, and helmet. To keep warm, he wore a white cape made of sheep's wool. The soldier himself was preparing to return home. At the gates of the city he came across a poor old beggar sitting on the ground, deep in the snow. At the sight of this, Martino came down from his horse, and with a quick blow of his sword, he cut his cloak in two and gave half to the poor old man so he may keep warm.

That night, Martino was awakened from an unexpected light. When he opened his eyes, he saw that before him stood Jesus wrapped in the half cloak that he had given to the old man. Martino jumped up full of joy and delight, Jesus had come to thank him! The young Roman soldier became a saint: Saint Martin, bishop of Tours.

Now we arrive at our holiday: the day of San Martino, the 11th of November. Venetian children, to remember the generous gesture of this saint, go around the city singing nursery rhymes and cheerfully banging on pots and pans, and playfully ask the shopkeepers and those who pass for a small gift. They receive sweets, candies, coins, but the fun is the best gift!

23

Let's play with Jacopo!

Nursery rhyme!

Let's sing together the nursery rhyme of San Martino, and then help Jacopo to reach his gift!

"San Martin xe andà in sofita
a trovar la so novissa,
la so novissa no ghe gera,
San Martin casca par tera!
E col nostro sachetin,
cari Signori xe San Martin!"

the solution is on page 120

24

The recipe of Marta

The traditional sweet of San Martino

Ingredients:
200 gr. of flour
100 gr. of sugar
100 gr. of butter
2 eggs
1/2 cup of water
pinch of salt

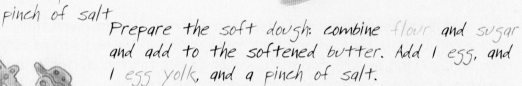

Prepare the soft dough: combine flour and sugar and add to the softened butter. Add 1 egg, and 1 egg yolk, and a pinch of salt.
Knead the dough water, adding in water, and let sit for 1/2 hour.
Meanwhile, prepare the outline of San Martino in cardboard, cut out the shape of the Saint on his horse with his sword and coat (like in the drawing).
Roll out the dough flat, and after, place the cardboard cut-out over the dough and cut out San Martino. Place in oven at 180° (350°F) and bake for 20 minutes. When it cools, you can decorate it melted chocolate, icing, chocolate bars, and candies.

25

2 - THE DISTRICTS

S. Giovanni e Paolo

Bragora

S. Zaccaria   Arsenale   Isola di S.Pietro

Pietà

CASTELLO

Riva degli Schiavoni   Giardini

Biennale

S. Elena

Castello is the most lively and populated district. It was given this name for a castle that, at one time, rose on the extreme point of city, facing Lido (the beach), for the defence of the first inhabitants that within this zone created and contributed to form the islands Realtine (around Rivoalto), the first unit of Venice.

Castello occupies the more eastern part of the city: towards the end, facing Lido, we find the island of S. Pietro, which was once called "Olivolo", from the olive trees that blossomed here: here stands the church of S. Pietro that from 775 was the seat of the first bishop of the Venetian population. In 1451 the bishop was given the title of Patriarch of Venice and since then, in the first half of 19th century (between 1800 and 1900), the seat was transferred to S. Marco.

ACCORDING TO TRADITION, THIS ANCIENT MARBLE CHAIR IS FOUND IN THE CHURCH OF SAN PIETRO, IT WAS USED BY THE SAINT. IT CAME TO BE CALLED "THE CHAIR OF S. PIETRO".

27

Up ahead we come to find the Arsenal, a gigantic construction of the most famous workshops, from which, produced and housed the commercial ships, and also ships of war, (galleys, trireme, galleons) which gave Venice its power and wealth. At one time, the Arsenal was surrounded and protected by a high wall, and from towers with the symbol of the winged lion.

Further up from the Arsenal we find the Public Gardens (I Giardini): this large green area, was wanted by Napoleon in 1807 as the city park, during a time that was alive with the bustle of fishermen and the pistori (bread makers), and the humble work of the merlettaie (lace makers) and of the impiraresse (threaders of glass pearls), typical occupations of Venetians (that nowadays are scarce).

The poet Dante came several to Venice.
When he visited the Arsenal, in 1321, as the ambassador of Guido Novello da Polenta, signore di Ravenna (Lord of Ravenna), he was so impressed by its power and frenetic activity, that he wrote of it in the 21st song of hell in his masterpiece, "The Divine Comedy".

THIS IS ONE OF THE TOWERS THAT
SURROUND THE ARSENAL: 4 MARBLE
LIONS GUARD ITS GATES, AND THAT
ONE DOWN THERE COMES FROM THE
ISLAND OF DELO.

29

In the district of Castello we find some of the most beautiful churches in the city: S. Giovanni and Paolo, was constructed in 1246 on a piece of land that was donated to the Dominican priests by the doge Jacopo Tiepolo, it was completed during the fourteenth century in gothic style; S. Giovanni in Bragora, was first established in the 8th century and was rebuilt in 1475, this was the church where Antonio Vivaldi was christened; the Pietà (S. Maria della Visitazione), an elegant church of 1700's, it was built where a an ancient orphanage once stood for children that were abandoned in the city; S. Zaccaria, was built in the 7th century, and contained the body of Saint Zaccaria, which was brought as a gift to the doge from Leo V the emperor of the Orient. Its bell tower is of the 12th century, is one of the most ancient of the town.

Today, a part of the Gardens of Castello is occupied by the Palace of the International Exposition of Modern Art. And since 1895 has been the home of the Biennial of Venice.

Here begins the long sidewalk of Riva degli Schiavoni that runs along the shoreline of the Bacino San Marco and ending at the Saint Mark Square.

THE CHIESA DELLA PIETA' ON THE RIVA DEGLI SCHIAVON

HEY, LULA, LOOK AT HOW VENICE
HAS THE FORM OF A FISH...!

31

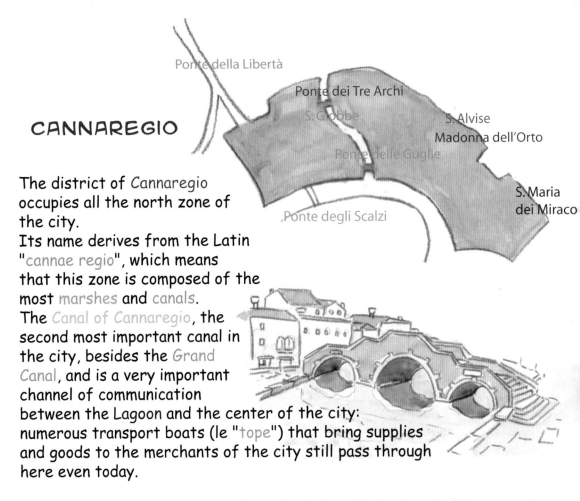

CANNAREGIO

The district of Cannaregio
occupies all the north zone of
the city.
Its name derives from the Latin
"cannae regio", which means
that this zone is composed of the
most marshes and canals.
The Canal of Cannaregio, the
second most important canal in
the city, besides the Grand
Canal, and is a very important
channel of communication
between the Lagoon and the center of the city:
numerous transport boats (le "tope") that bring supplies
and goods to the merchants of the city still pass through
here even today.

The two fondamenta that run along the sides of the Canal of Cannaregio
are connected by two bridges: Bridge of the Needles, that received its
name for the 4 stone needles (2 on either side) placed
along the bridge, and Bridge of Three Arcs, characterized by its 3 arcs
that are constrcted at the base of the bridge that boats pass
through when entering or exiting the Lagoon.

32

HERE I AM!
THIS IS THE **PONTE DELLE GUGLIE**
THAT CROSSES THE **CANALE DI CANNAREGIO**.
IN FRONT OF ME IS THE FONDAMENTA THAT IS
THE HEBREW QUARTERS CALLED GHETTO,
IT IS HERE THAT THERE ARE THE **HIGHEST HOUSES**
IN THE CITY!

Strolling through Cannaregio we can visit some attractive and ancient churches of Venice:

S. Maria dei Miracoli, covered on all sides in eastern marble, constructed and inlaid with great art and fantasy;

S. Alvise, of gothic architecture, was erected in one of the loneliest and most isolated places in the city, wanted by a Venetian noblewoman in 1383, when S. Luigi d'Angiò, S. Alvise in dialect, appeared before her in a dream. Inside this church hang 3 masterpieces of Giambattista Tiepolo;

S. MARIA DEI MIRACOLI

S. ALVISE

Madonna dell'Orto, has an attractive medieval facade of red brick, and was given its name when an image of Madonna col Bambino (the Virgin Mary) was miraculously found in a garden and brought into the church by the devotion of the people. It is the birth parish of the great painter Tintoretto; it is in this church, that they take care of 3 of his masterpieces.

S. Giobbe is one of the first examples of renaissance architecture in Venice, it emphasized by its elegant and refined main entrance, a work of art by Pietro Lombardo.

MADONNA DELL'ORTO

S. GIOBBE

35

The Ghetto

On the right hand side of the Canale di Cannaregio, beyond the ponte delle Guglie, we visit the Ghetto, a Jewish district from 1527 by disposition of the Signoria (Venetian tribunal) and is still today inhabited from the Jewish community: here, in campo del Ghetto, you can visit the synagogue and pass between the shops characteristic of this community, and visit the bakery where you can buy a typical Jewish sweet.

If we look up we notice that the houses here are really very high, in respect to the rest of the city: being that the Ghetto was a closed district for many years, the only way of providing for more space was by building upwards. Some buildings have up to 8 floors!

THE NAME GHETTO WAS COINED
IN VENICE.
DUE TO THE MANY FOUNDREYS
IN THIS ZONE THAT HAD TO
"GETTARE" (MELT) METALS;
THIS NAME WAS THEN ADAPTED
ALL OVER THE WORLD AS A
TERM TO INDICATE A JEWISH
COMMUNITY.

Stazione Marittima
S. Marta
S. Nicolò dei Mendicoli
I Carmini
S. Sebastiano
S. Trovaso
Salute
Fondamenta delle Zattere

DORSODURO

Dorsoduro is the southern district of the city, a long strip that begins at Punta della Dogana (Customs Point) and runs until the Maritime Station of S. Marta.
Most likely, it received its name for the particular type of stony ground, "dossi", that is present only in that area.

The southern boundary of Dorsoduro is marked by the sunny fondamenta delle Zattere, which runs along the Canal of Giudecca from S. Basilio until the Punta della Dogana.

This long tree-lined avenue allows all who stroll along it to enjoy the beautiful views of the other side of the Canal, from the Palladian churches of Zitelle and Redentore, to the islands of Giudecca and S. Giorgio.

DO YOU KNOW WHY THIS FONDAMENTA
IS CALLED ZATTERE?

BECAUSE MANY YEARS AGO THEY WOULD
BRING ASHORE THE "GROSSE ZATTERE"
(LARGE WOODEN RAFTS),
THAT WERE NAVIGATED DOWN THE
RIVERS, OF TRUNKS THAT FELL
FROM THE MOUNTAINS, AND THE
TIMBER WAS THEN USED
FOR ITS NEED IN THE CITY.

39

In the heart of the district of Dorsoduro, we find Campo Santa Margherita, one of the largest and most populated campos in the city. It is also the meeting place for young adults during the summer evenings. In the center of the campo stands an isolated building, the ancient Scuola dei Varoteri (fur trader).

In front of this school there are two medieval palaces, although built during different periods, they are similar in that they have a brick face and a protruding roof, a rarity in Venice.

ON THE WALL OF THE SCUOLA DEI VAROTERI (SCHOOL OF THE VAROTERI) THERE IS A PLAQUE, FROM THE SERENISSIMA, THAT STATES THE MINIMUM MEASURE OF FISH THAT CAN BE SOLD IN THE MARKET.

To the back of the campo, towards Zattere, we find the Scuola di Santa Maria del Carmine, one of the 6 Scuole Grandi (see page 50), designed by B. Longhena in 1600. Inside the school there are masterpieces of G.B. Tiepolo and other important Venetian painters of the 1700's.

The district of Dorsoduro is not lacking in beautiful churches to visit:

S. Nicolò dei Mendicoli rises on the island Mendigola, seat of an ancient and important community devoted to fishing, and those whom authorized the election of an actual doge, "small doge of the Nicolotti" (you will see the two groups of the Nicolotti and Castellani in "A Story of Grandfather Bepi", on page 56). This church was founded in the 7th century, and is the second most ancient in the city, after S. Giacometto di Rialto.

San Sebastiano (that can be seen on the rio of S. Basilio, little before Zattere), is interesting, not only that for its meticulous architecture, typical of the Renaissance, but above all, for the spectacular pictorial cycle* of Paolo Veronese inside the church. The painter, that is buried here, worked in this church for 15 years, from 1551 to 1565;

*a series of works of the same painter, at times they share the same theme or subject matter.

42

San Trovaso, dedicated to the saints Gervasio and Protasio (which has become Trovaso), preserves inside of it, a cloth of Jacopo Tintoretto representing The Last Supper, subject most represented by this Venetian painter;

I Carmini, a gothic church, was built in 1386 by the Carmelitani monks;

Santa Maria della Salute was built as a worship temple dedicated to the Virgin to give thanks for the end of the plague of 1630 (see page 92). The church, designed by B. Longhena, has a shape of a "crown", similar to the crown of Maria, symbol of victory. The location of the church is in the center of Bacino San Marco, facing all three Palladian churches: Redentore, Zitelle, and S. Giorgio. The gigantic dome and the high stairs, is typical of the Baroque style.

43

S. POLO AND S. CROCE

S. Polo and S. Croce are two central districts, those of whose boundaries are interwoven one into the other one, and intersect themselves continuously. This is a very lively zone, the beating heart of the city life, these two districts contain actual mazes of streets (calli) and narrow side streets (callette), bridges (ponti) and channels (canali), shortcuts (corti sconte), tunnels (sottoportici) that emerge in small hidden courtyards (campielli), houses (case) and shops (botteghe) that developed throughout the centuries.

S.Giacometto
S.Polo
S. Zan Degolà   S.Maria Gloriosa dei Frari
S.Rocco
S.Giacomo dell'Orio

The "campi" mark the stops along the walk in this center of Venice; they open themselves unexpectedly when you are re-emerging from its maze, finally allowing you to recollect yourself and sweep a look at the surroundings.
It is typically advised to follow the path of Campo S. Rocco, Campo S. Tomà, Campo dei Frari, Campo S. Polo, and finishing at Rialto, the true center of the city.

44

The zone of Rialto, of the ancient islands Realtine, was the seat of the government from 811, and the seat of all merchant trafficking of the Serenissima. This zone is the heart of the city life: the wide and busy street the Ruga Rialto, that is lined with one thousand shops in frantic activity, and leads us to the beginning of the market, with a multitude of colored stands selling fruit and vegetables in Campo dell'Erbaria and the Pescaria, arranged under the covered protection of the spacious columns.

The market of Rialto is a unforgettable spectacle: people of every age that go around from one stand to the next with their carts, the sellers yelling to publicize their prices and products, the colors, smells, voices, sounds: Venice, more alive than ever!

45

These two small districts of the city center also offer certain attractive churches to visit, some of these are:

Pala dell'Assunta

S. Giovanni Battista

coro ligneo

Basilica di
S. Maria Gloriosa
dei Frari

Pala Pesaro

The Franciscan monks, arrived in Venice in 1222, and lived their first years in poverty, in small huts, preaching the evangelic message of S. Francesco. Their reputation began with the doge Jacopo Tiepolo, who in 1250 gave them this land on which to build their first church (smaller than the present one and designed in an opposite sense). Seeing as the monks were developing a large following, the need to build a new church was imminent, and so they constructed the present church, in gothic style, and it was consecrated in 1330.

46

The facade is much to Franciscan taste, somber, airy and light with its large central rosette. The plan of the church is a Latin cross. The nave is route from strong pillars that sustain the acute arcs and at times crisscross, typical of gothic style.

On the inside of the church there are works of art by many famous artists. Of these, not to miss, are the two paintings by Tiziano Vecellio: la Pala dell'Assunta (1518), which is located on the main altar. To the left of the side entrance is Pala Pesaro, commissioned by the noble and rich Venetian family Pesaro; the wooden choir inlays, are divided in three orders with 124 places from where the monks prayed and song;

the Trittico*
of the Madonna e
Santi (Madonna
and Saints) on
the altar of
Cappella Pesaro
by Giovanni Bellini
in 1488; the
wooden statue
of S. Giovanni
Battista of
Donatello,
Florentine artist
that came to Venice in 1438.

*work of art divided in three different zones

S. Giacomo di Rialto

The church S. Giacomo di Rialto, familiarly called S. Giacometto by Venetians, is traditionally known as the most ancient of the city: it was established in the 5th century, when the first inhabitants arrived on the Realtine islands.

The actual structure dates back to the 11th century, contemporary to the market of Rialto, and was restored around 1600.

It is one of the few examples of Romanesque architecture in Venice, in a style called Venetian-Byzantine.

In front of the facade there is a gothic open gallery, with columns made of stone and the buttress of wood: is the only authentic example remaining in Venice (other than S. Nicolò dei Mendicoli which is a reconstruction).

The Hunchback of Rialto, named for the folded statue that supports the stairs, it is found directly in front of the church; it is the column of the exile, from which the Signoria stood to read the exiles, proclamations, condemnations, etc.

48

S. Zan Degolà

The church, dedicated to S. Giovanni Decollato (in Venetian, S. Zan Degolà) was erected by the expenditures of the rich Venier family in 1007, in a lonely zone of the small archipelago of S. Croce. Although it had been restored various times, it did not lose the typical Venetian-Byzantine structure, common to the most ancient churches of Venice.

On the inside there are many frescos of the Byzantine school of the 13th century, rare evidence of the Eastern pictorial technology, which was unknown to the West.

S. Giacomo dell'Orio

This is an ancient church, founded in the 9th century and rebuilt in 1225. Of this period remains the majestic bell tower, which is a remembrance of the cathedral of Torcello.
The inside is a merger of the romanesque and gothic languages. Looking at the columns, you can see that one in particular is more beautiful than the others; it is made of green granite with many grains. It arrived from Bisanzio, perhaps it belonged to a previous construction and it was re-used in the construction of the church.

49

Scuola Grande di S. Rocco

Near to Frari, facing the absidi* of the church, is the Campo S. Rocco.

Here in this campo, besides the church dedicated to the saint who is the protector of the patients of the plague, we can find the Scuola Grande di S. Rocco: the Scuole Grandi (Large Schools), 6 in all, were religious institute associations of the Serenissima designed to help the poor during scarcities, wars, or pestilences; between the richest and most noble members of the confraternity one "Guardian Grande" ("Large Guardian") was elected, the most high office, granted still today.

The inside of the Scuola Grande di S. Rocco is literally covered with more than 40 large canvases of Jacopo Tintoretto.

In 1564, in fact, a competition was announced to choose the artist that would paint the central panel of the ceiling of the Sala dell'Albergo della Scuola: with large annoyance of his long time rival, Paolo Veronese, the famous Tintoretto arranged his works in their places, which were already finished, but which were still to be judged. It was in this way, that not only was he ordered the decoration of the walls and of the ceiling, but also he was made honorary member of the School.

For 23 years he decorated the whole building with a sole cycle of painting for spectacularity, beauty, and spirituality.

*opposite part the facade of a church

51

Campo S. Tomà

A short distance from Frari there is the Campo S. Tomà, with an ancient church and very particular sailing bell tower: Grandfather Bepi says that the customers started with a very ambitious project, and shortly after the beginning of the intense work, they realized they didn't have enough money required to finish the construction, so they were forced to abandon the project and leave an incomplete bell tower, like the sail of a boat, which can be seen today. Opposite of this there is the ancient Scuoletta dei Calegheri (shoemakers). The art of the Shoemakers (l'Arte dei Calegheri), in the church of S. Tomà there was an actual altar dedicated to S. Mark, where every year a gift was offered to the duchess, a pair of clogs.

SAILING BELLTOWER IN CAMPO S. TOMA'

Up ahead, after the bridge of S. Tomà, we find the Palace Centani: with an attractive gothic facade, the small courtyard with a well, a traditional outside staircase that was covered by the roof (of which few remain), very refined angles,and Venetian composure.

Here, in 1707, the famous comedy writer Carlo Goldoni was born, one the most eminent citizens of Venice.

The genius of Carlo Goldoni lives on still today in his works, from "I quattro rusteghi" to "La Locandiera", from "The campiello" to "Arlecchino servitore di due padroni" , still performed in theaters, giving life his characters that are typically Venetians and deeply human: unforgettable characters like the gruff Lunardo, the ingenuous fake Lucietta, Sior Todaro brontolon.

House of Goldoni (Casa Goldoni) is used today as a Museum of the Theater and preserves the memories of the life of the comedy writer, and the precious depositions of the theater and of the costumes of the 1700's.

SURELY YOU NOTICED THAT BETWEEN THE DISTRICTS WE STILL HAVE NOT SEEN SAN MARCO
DON'T WORRY, IT IS COMING UP IN THE NEXT CHAPTER.

MEANWHILE LET'S TAKE A LITTLE REST, AND NOW GRANDFATHER WILL TELL US A STORY.

COME ON JACOPO, COME UP, IT'S STARTING!

A story of Grandfather Bepi

The bridge of the Fists

Listen up kids, this story brings us far back in the time when Venice was divided in two opposite groups (gangs), one from either side of the Grand canal; the Castellani and the Nicolotti. The first is of the district of S. Pietro di Castello, the second, instead, is of the opposite part of the town, S. Nicolò dei Mendicoli in Dorsoduro. It once was that when a group of Nicolotti met a group of Castellani they began shouting insults, then evolved to fist fights, and finally blind blows... The doge, attentive to the decorum and to the civil cohabitation of its citizens, sought to resolve this matter and calm these quarrelsome youngsters, which resulted in a new decree: they were able to fight for holy reasons, but only once per year, during the parties of carnival.

They chose between themselves where to have this fight, on a bridge near S. Barnaba it could have been a theater of this playful struggle: the gang that succeeded in crossing to the other side of the bridge while withstanding pushes and punches from the other gang carried home the victory, valid for all year. Naturally, the losers were those who ended up in the water, between the yells and the passionate fans of the crowds on either side of the canal.

56

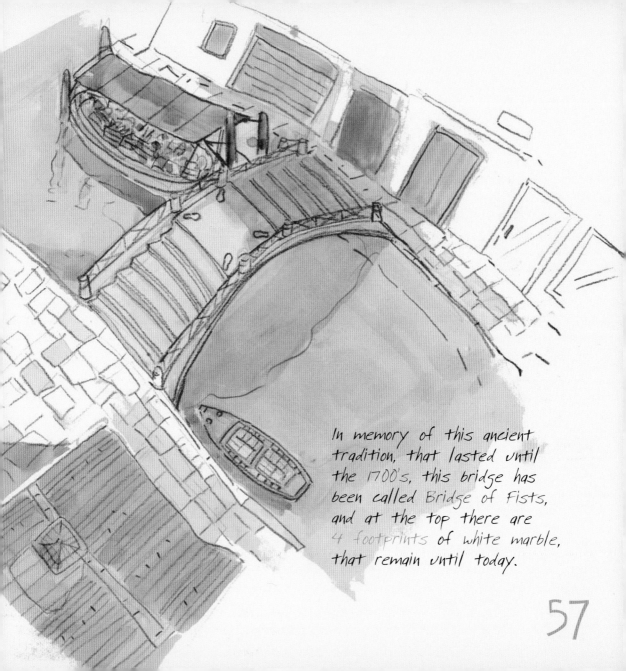

In memory of this ancient
tradition, that lasted until
the 1700's, this bridge has
been called Bridge of Fists,
and at the top there are
4 footprints of white marble,
that remain until today.

57

Let's play with Jacopo!
The Grand Canal
on a penholder

What you'll need:
a roll of cardboard
green paper
blue paper
white paper
glue
scissors
felt-tip pen

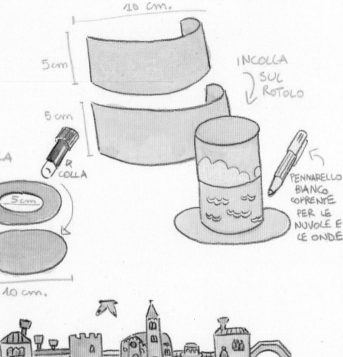

PERFETTO

10 cm.

5 cm

INCOLLA SUL ROTOLO

5 cm

COLLA

PENNARELLO BIANCO COPRENTE PER LE NUVOLE E LE ONDE

ROTOLO

INCOLLA

5 cm

10 cm.

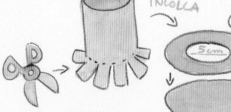

DISEGNA LE CASE E RITAGLIA LUNGO I BORDI

DISEGNA BARCHE E BRICOLE

INCOLLA I DISEGNI TAGLIATI SUL PORTAPENNE!

58

The recipe of Marta
The Venetian Zaleti

Ingredients:
200 gr. of flour type 00
200 gr. of yellow flour
150 gr. of sugar
120 gr. of butter
150 gr. of raisins
5 egg yolks
baking powder
a pinch of salt
powdered sugar

Blend together the two flours, and then add the butter (room temperature). Beat egg yolks and sugar together with a beater and add raisins, salt, and baking powder. Taking small pieces at a time roll the dough into the shape of small bread rolls and bake in the oven at 180° for 15 minutes.

When they have cooled, cover them with the powdered sugar... a great afternoon snack!

59

3 - SAINT MARK

ponte di Rialto

Piazza S. Marco

ponte dell'Accademia

Saint. Mark, the center of art, history and culture in the city, and has been the primitive unit of Venice, together with Rialto and San Pietro di Castello. The evangelist Mark became Patron of the town in the year 829, when his body and belongings were carried to Venice from Alessandria of Egypt (see page 78): next to the Castle of the Doge (Castello del Doge), called the Doge's Palace (Palazzo Ducale), a new church was erected, the Doge's Chapel (Cappella Ducale) and was dedicated to Saint Mark.

This zone became immediately the heart of the town and here the noble families began building their palaces, together with the doge, hereby combining hand in hand the government and the economy of the city.

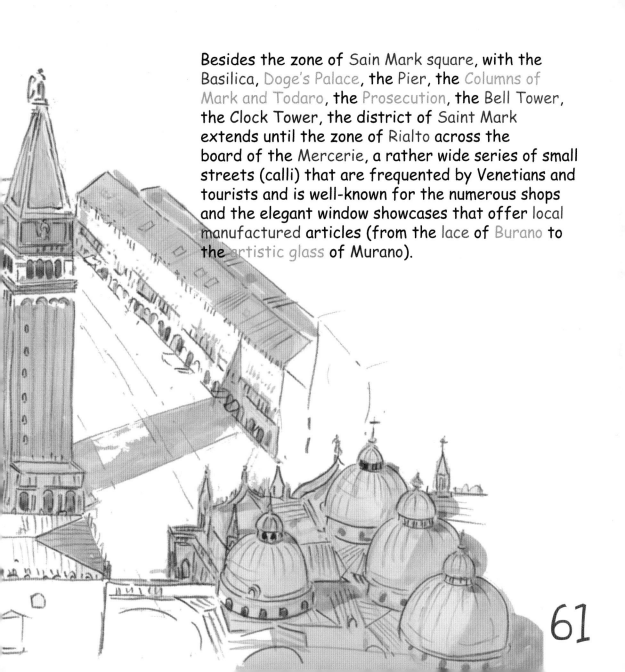

Besides the zone of Sain Mark square, with the Basilica, Doge's Palace, the Pier, the Columns of Mark and Todaro, the Prosecution, the Bell Tower, the Clock Tower, the district of Saint Mark extends until the zone of Rialto across the board of the Mercerie, a rather wide series of small streets (calli) that are frequented by Venetians and tourists and is well-known for the numerous shops and the elegant window showcases that offer local manufactured articles (from the lace of Burano to the artistic glass of Murano).

SAINT MARK SQUARE

Here we are in Saint Mark Square, living room of the world! The ancient Caffè Quadri and Florian, the Liston*, the orchestras that invite you to waltz, the flying dance of the pigeons: the atmosphere is really magical!

But let's look around: the Square, 175 meters long, and 82 meters wide from the part of the Basilica and 57 meters on the opposite side, and was paved in terracotta in 1267: first there were trees and grassy earth, and was called "brolo", which means "garden".
The pavement that we see today is constructed in tiles of trachyte, with drawings in white stone, which dates back to 1723.

Two sides of the Square are occupied by the Prosecutors (Procuratie), so called this because here resided the prosecutors of Saaint Mark. On the third side, facing the Basilica, stands the church of S. Geminiano. In 1807 Napoleon demolished the building to construct a ballroom near the Palazzo Reale: imagine the protests of the citizens! Today in this wing of the Square there are the rooms of the Museum Correr (Museo Correr).

62

*a walk along the Square following the line in white stone (strip)

BASILICA OF SAINT MARK

On the 4th side of the Piazza, stands the Basilica of S. Mark.
When the body of Saint Mark was brought to Venice from Alessandria
of Egypt in the year 829, he was proclaimed patron of the city, and thus
began the construction of the first basilica.
The building however, was destroyed in a fire, but was immediately
rebuilt under the governmental rule of the doge Pietro Orseolo II, in 978.
The Venetians, seeing the growth of their power, reputation, and wealth,
under the influence of the artistic fervor and religion, that was
influenced by the East around the year 1000, decided to renew their
church and to rebuild it larger and more beautiful.
They demolished the old church of Saint Mark and closed the church
of S. Teodoro, and began the construction of the third Basilica of
S. Mark, the one we see today, which was consecrated in 1094 under
the doge Vitale Falier.

The design of the Basilica is like that of the Greek cross, with 5 domes and an architecture faithful to the eastern style, Greek-Byzantine. The constant work of embellishment of the church lasted for centuries: they immediately began the mosaic decoration and the marble coverings with materials and manpower more common of the East.

On the angle of the Basilica, towards the pier, we find the Tetrarchi, a group of sculptures in porphyry from the 6th century, brought to Venice from the East, like many other sculptures and decorations of the church.
The group represented is that of Augusti and Cesari united in the government of the Empire: a popular legend says that these 4 figures are the 4 dark-skinned petrified men that tried to steal the Treasure of S. Mark!

The inside of the Basilica is all of sparkling gold, covered with more than 4000 square meters of mosaics!
The game of the colors and the riches of the decorations create an almost unreal atmosphere of solemn magnificence.
They come to tell the stories of the life of Jesus and the Old Testament, like a gigantic illustrated Bible!
Some parts are dedicated to the stories of the lives of various saints, and of S. Mark and his miraculous arrival to Venice.

64

On the first altar to left we stop to look at the Madonna Nicopeja, an icon of 10th century, transported to Venice from Constantinople like war booty and has been present in the Basilica since 1234: and during the centuries has become a small pilgrimage for many Venetians and foreigners alike.

The cathedral of Saint Mark is truly a treasure chest to discover: between these, is the striking crypt*, where until a few years ago, contained the body of the evangelist S. Mark (which now is located under the main altar in the basilica) the Pala d'Oro (the Shovel of Gold), shining with jewellery that was set with artistic beauty, and 4 bronze horses adorning the facade (these are a copy of the originals that were brought from Constantinople in 1204: those of which can be found in the museum of the Treasury of Saint Mark , the pavement, was designed from thousands of tiles in marble, porphyry, and glass.

*Small underground church that welcomed the body of the Martyr and the relics of the saint.

65

THE PIER

The Pier is the water entrance to Saint Mark Square: once the ships from the East brought merchandise and war booty to the city, and these were welcomed and honored by the Venetians. To protect this entrance to Venice, two columns of granite were constructed, carried from Greece in the 12th century, and were dedicated to S. Teodoro and S. Mark, patrons of the city: during their disembarkment, one of three original columns fell into the water and it was never possible to recover it.

The Lion of Saint Mark is made of bronze and was placed on of the column dedicated to S. Mark, in reality it is a statue of eastern influence that represents a chimera (a fantastic animal), to which wings were added to disguise it as the winged lion. In fact, if we look at well, the "Lion" it has almond eyes and the mouth of a dragon!

THE CLOCKTOWER

The Clock Tower is one of the most famous elements of Saint Mark Square: it is the largest astronomical clock, which for more than 500 years has told the time, and also told of the life and of the story of Venice.
It was inaugurated in 1499 "above the mouth of Marzaria", that is to say that it marks the entrance of the most important road that leads from the Square to the historic Merceria.

With its recent restorations the inside mechanism was replaced and now functions correctly, a masterpiece of technology and engineering: it is interesting to visit, upon reservation, the inside of the tower and the small rooms that accommodate the mechanisms of clock, ascending to the top where the two bronze statues of the dark men beat the bell every hour.

Twice per year, the day of "Epifania" and "Ascensione", the Wise Men exit every hour from the center of the tower, and bow themselves to Maria and Child and re-enter from the same part. It is a fantastic show, not to miss!

67

THE BELLTOWER

The bell tower of S. Mark, entirely detached from the Basilica, was begun in 888, and was continued to be built until the 14th century.

It is called by the Venetians "el paron de casa" (the owner of the house), because is the highest of all of the bell towers of Venice: 98.60 meters. From the top of the high tower, one can admire the spectacular view of the city: a mosaic of a thousand colors, roofs, chimneys, covered roof terraces campi, channels, calli and bridges...

Many famous people, in the course of the centuries, have climbed the great tower: one of these is Galileo, who demonstrated to the governors of the Serenissima in 1609 the wonders of his telescope.

But, look her: July 14, 1902 the bell tower suddenly crumbles down upon itself. Fortunately, no one was hurt! Of the 5 bells, alone it "Marangona" was found unbroken between the rubble.

The new bell tower, the one we see today, was inaugurated on April 25, 1912, the day of S. Mark. And it had been decided, that was "com'era, dov'era" (what once was, where once was).

By the way, do you guys know in Venice it is used "un'ombra" (a shadow) to indicate a glass of wine?

Because, once the selling stand of wine was located directly under the Bell Tower, and to keep the wine cool, it was positioned always in the shadow of the tower!

THE DOGE'S PALACE

The Doge's Palace, seat of the doge and of the highest offices of the Serenissima, and was the only building for a long time to be called a Palace (the other was called simply ca', diminutive of house).
It was founded in the year 814 under the doge Angelo Partecipazio: it was originally a fortified castle, with a battlemented wall, and ditches and angular towers of medieval type.
This antique castle was built to defend invasions from the Lombards of the king Rotari, but there remains no evidence of this.
In the 14th and 15th century this building was destroyed by various fires, and was replaced with the building that we see today: the entire Palace leans on a porch sustained by columns, its front is constructed in marble from Verona, and its arcs are like embroideries of lace: a true masterpiece of gothic architecture.
On the inside of the Palace, the power of the Serenissima is emphasized, the entire Palace was planned to impress and frighten the ambassadors, the king, and the dignified who came to visit to the doge. Inside the rooms there are, highs seats of inlaid wood, enriched with adorned stucco, and with canvasses by the most famous artists of the era; the gilded staircases to the ceilings, the inside courtyards that contain enormous statues to indicate to the visitor the power of the Serenissima.
The route, told by the Secret Itineraries, that brings you from a hidden room in the Palace to the Inquisition Room, and to the lobby of the Chancellery, ending at the Prisons: it is possible to have this visit, but only upon reservation, and is really interesting!

A Story
of Grandfather Bepi

The Bud of Saint Mark

This story will take us to Venice during
the time of the Crusades. In the district
of S. Croce, there lived an attractive girl named
Colombina, who belonged to the noblest family in the city.
Giovanni, her fiancé, that she could not wait to marry, decided
to depart for the war to become a courageous knight and to
return Venice full of pride and honor, to respectably take
the hand of the beautiful Colombina.
One day the Venetians, led by the doge Enrico Dandolo, were
about to join the Crusades and were departing for the East
to join the war against the Sultan of Egypt: what better
occasion?
Horse, armour, sword, and shield, there stood Giovanni in line
with the other knights in departure from Venice: it was 1204,
and the beginning of the Fourth Crusade.
Immediately in Venice, news began arriving of the numerous
victories of the Venetians and it was told they had gained
the entire capital Eastern Empire, Constantinople.

72

Colombina waited for her courageous knight with great trepidation. It was known that the *doge* and his men had returned from the *East* loaded with gold, and of conquests and honors.
Colombina come down to the *Pier* (Molo di San Marco) in a hurry, where the soldiers were disembarking from the *Crusades*: with her eyes, she searched and searched everyface in the crowd to find that of *Giovanni*, but did not succeed in finding him. In that moment, a soldier approached her and delivered to her a *red rose*.
Giovanni, had left for reasons of love, but he had been injured in battle, and while he lay dying, he dyed the *white rose* that he had picked for his *Colombina* red with his blood.

For this reason, still today, in Venice, *April 25*, the day of S. Mark, the men of the city give their loved one a red rose bud, *il bò'colo*.

73

Let's play with Jacopo!

The Mosaic

That in which you see below is the face of San Marco, in a mosaic in the Basilica.
Try to follow the picture and color it! But if you want to make the actual mosaic, enlarge the drawing with a photocopier, and recover it using pieces of colored paper (even if clipped from a magazine). Good Job!

74

The recipe of Marta

1 Baicoli

Ingredients:
500 gr. of flour
50 gr. of butter
50 gr. of sugar
15 gr. of beer yeast
1 egg
milk
salt

First blend the flour with the sugar and unite with softened butter and 1 egg white (whipped like snow), add in the yeast and a little warm milk and a pinch of salt.
Work the dough continuously, and keep adding milk until you have firm dough. After you have left it to rise for 2 hours, divide it into small loaves of bread and place on a greased baking sheet, and let sit to rise for another 1 1/2 hours.
Put in oven and bake at 180° for 15 minutes. Let sit for 2 days, and finish by slicing the sweets very thin and slanting.

Before serving them, toast the baicoli slightly in a warm oven.

75

4 - VENICE AND ITS STORY

HOW WAS VENICE BORN?

Tradition tells us that Venice was been founded in the
year 421.
We know however, that since the times of the
Roman Empire, during the first centuries of
Christianity, in the lagoon islands of the Adriatic
coast, between sandy and earthy, swampy
dunes, there lived small groups of fishermen,
hunters, and boatmen. With the intensifying
barbaric invasions, between the 5th and 7th century,
the population of the flourishing cities of the Veneto
region began fleeing and seeking refuge the coastal
lagoons, lonely and protected. This is how these islands
became increasingly populated, enriching itself with
inhabitants, therefore of traffic and of commerce.

And little by little, while the terrible Huns, driven from Attila, spread
fear across the mainland, and upon the Lombard's, a short distance away,
the population formed in the Venetian lagoons a true and actual Byzantine
province governed by the maritime tribunes, after replaced by the office
of a duke, called in Venetian "doge".

This province was constructed from innumerable small islands and from the three greater of Grado, seat of the bishop; Torcello, center and crossroad of all deals and commerce; Malamocco, seat of the government.

Later on, facing new dangers coming from the sea, the doge transferred his residence to the group of internal islands, more protected, isole di Rivoaltus, the current zone of Rialto, where little by little grew a new city: Venice!

WHY IS SAINT MARK
THE PATRON OF VENICE?

According to tradition, the body and belongings of
S. Mark the Evangelist had been carried back to Venice,
with shrewdness, from Alexandria of Egypt by Venetian
merchants, in the year 829.

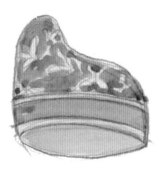

The possession of the body of the saint, came with
the help of two monks, the merchants Buono da
Malamocco and Rustico da Torcello, who hid it in a
basket and covered it with pork, which is considered
impure by Muslims, and so was passed easily through
customs and controls.

Their arrival in Venice had been welcomed with a large party held by the bishop Orso and the doge Giustiniano Particiaco. It was January 31, 829. S. Mark was proclaimed patron of the city, together with S. Teodoro. Teodoro, a Greek saint was already chosen as the protector of Venice by the emperor of the East. In honor of the new Venetian patron, the first Basilica was erected Basilica of Saint Mark, next to the Castle of Doge.

After a fire that destroyed the first church, the body of Saint Mark was found miraculously untouched, the body was then placed, with every honor, in the new Basilica, in 1094.

QUEEN OF THE ADRIATIC

Around the year 1000, Venice lived a period of great splendor:
the development commercial traffic, of commerce, of the
navigational increase in authority, power, and riches.
Under the doge Pietro Orseolo II, the Venetians gained at
all costs the Dalmazia, opening itself to the Eastern road.

It is actually in this occasion than Venice received the title
of Queen of the Adriatic, and began the solemn ceremony of
the Wedding of the Sea: which Grandfather Bepi will tell us
in the next story (page 86)!

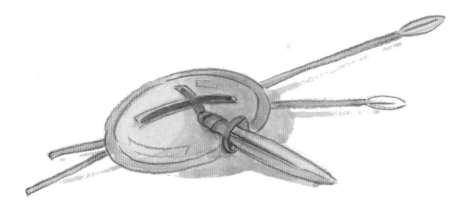

Other events that mark
the growth of Venice
are the victories over
the terrible Normans that
threatened not only the
Adriatic Sea, but also
the powerful Empire
of the East.

The Venetians, by means
of having powerful and
numerous fleets of war
ships, succeeded to hunt
the Normans and thus
gaining large honors by
the Byzantine Empire, but
above all commercial ease.
The port of Venice became
the most important European
port in all or Europe, and the
obligated passage for
commerce between
Europe and the East.

VENICE AND THE CRUSADES

Under the rule of the doge Enrico Dandolo, at the end of the 12th century, Venice is at its height of the power and splendor: the Arsenal (see page 28) succeeds to build one ship of war* per day!
In view of new conquests, in 1204 the doge decided to unite his fleet in the Fourth Crusade in departure for Egypt, against the sultan and his army.
During their travels, in agreement with the crusaders, they become deviated towards the Byzantine Empire: Constantinople is besieged and gained. Venice comes in possession of a fourth of the Eastern Empire and an immense war booty.

Of the enormous riches in gold, jewellery, works of art that the Venetians carry triumphantly at home, they also bring the 4 bronze horses that are placed above the arc of the entrance of the Basilica of S. Mark.

*The trireme is the Venetian ship of war most dreadful: every ship has 150 rowers divided into groups of three, synchronized by a drum beat that gives them the rhythm to row. At the bow there was a sharpened bundle and cannon, which served to sink the hostile ships.

IL DOGE

The doge, which means duke, leader, was the greatest authority of the Venetian State.

From the birth of Venice, as we saw, the islands of the Lagoon were a province of the Eastern Empire, governed by the maritime tribunes. With the acquisition of their independence from Byzantium (capital of the Eastern Empire), the government was passed to a duke or doge, elected first with the approval of the Eastern Emperor, then from the noble Venetians that we part of the Greater Advice.

The doge, that remained in office for life, and his advisors, the Advice of Ten (Consiglio dei Dieci), became elected by 2.000 members of the Greater Advice. During the election, they did not lack rivalry, personal interest and gain, plays of power and abuses of power.

There have been a total of 120 doges that have governed Venice: the first one was Paoluccio Anafesto, elected in 697.

Some other important figures of the dogi that remained in historical memory for their greatness:

Pietro Orseolo II, under whom the kingdom of Venice became Queen of the Seas;

Sebastiano Ziani, in 1177 hosted both the pope Alessandro III and the emperor Federico Barbarossa at Doge's Palace, who came to Venice for reconciliation;

Enrico Dandolo, as we read, participated in the 4th Crusades until the age of 90, and conquered Constantinople;

And the last of the dogi was Ludovico Manin, whose rule concluded with the fall of the Serenissima to the Austrians in 1797.

HEY LULA, LOOK: HOW DO I LOOK WITH THIS "ZOGIA"? DO I SEEM A TRUE DOGE?

85

A story of Grandfather Bepi

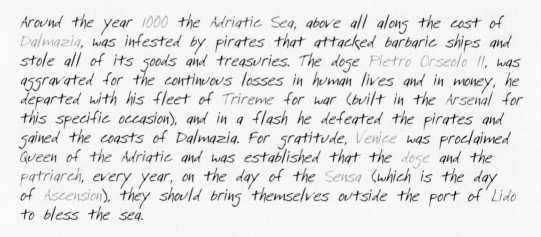

The Wedding of the Sea

Hey kids, sit and listen to this story, which will bring us on the sea, on board of the legendary ship of the doge, the Bucintoro.

Around the year 1000 the Adriatic Sea, above all along the cost of Dalmazia, was infested by pirates that attacked barbaric ships and stole all of its goods and treasuries. The doge Pietro Orseolo II, was aggravated for the continuous losses in human lives and in money, he departed with his fleet of Trireme for war (built in the Arsenal for this specific occasion), and in a flash he defeated the pirates and gained the coasts of Dalmazia. For gratitude, Venice was proclaimed Queen of the Adriatic and was established that the doge and the patriarch, every year, on the day of the Sensa (which is the day of Ascension), they should bring themselves outside the port of Lido to bless the sea.

But most beautiful part holiday was added later: pope Alessandro III recognized the importance of the peace that the doge made with the emperor Federico Barbarossa, and he gave to Venice a ring of gold, a symbol of its union with the sea. This began the traditionally Wedding of the Sea, which lasted for centuries, until the fall of the Serenissima, in 1797.

On the day of the Sensa, the party was extravagant: the doge climbed onto his ship, the Bucintoro, with the blessings of everyone. Behind him was an immense procession of boats in every form and color.

On the topsail of the Bucintoro waved the banner ducal, and the admiral of the Arsenal gave orders to his men to set sail for the port of Lido.
Before the Forte di S. Andrea the patriarch solemnly poured holy water into the sea. Then the doge, from a window on the stern of the Bucintoro, threw a ring of gold into the sea, and called out: "We marry you, O Sea, as token of eternal dominion!".

With this lavish ceremony, began the Fiera della Sensa: with parties, shows, stands, and storytelling, which lasted for days in Venice. Over the last few years, it was decided to back this historical ritual of the Wedding to the Sea: it is a true jump into the past, during the splendor of the Serenissima.

Let's play with Jacopo!

Quiz...together!

Are you ready, have you memorized well
the story of Venice? Ok then, let's go!

1 - What are the names of the three most important
islands of the Lagoon before the birth of Venice?

2 - Who was the first doge of Venice?

3 - What is the name of the city from which
the body of S. Mark was taken and
carried back to Venice?

4 - Which of the crusades did the Venetians
participate? Who was the doge that
led them?

Did you do it? Great job! Compare you
answers to those on page 120

The recipe of Marta

The Kisses in Gondola

Ingredients:
130 gr. of flour
150 gr. of almonds
150 gr. of sugar
50 gr. of melted chocolate
100 gr. of butter

Add together sugar, flour, softened butter and minced almonds. Mix well and when you have obtained a well-blended mixture, begin to form small balls of dough, slightly pressed down. Place them on a greased baking sheet let cook for 15 minutes and medium temperature. Take out of oven and let cool.

Meanwhile melt the chocolate. Spread chocolate mixture on flat side of one cookie and add another half on top (like a sandwich). Let cool, and they will unite with "a kiss"!

89

5 - HOLIDAYS AND TRADITIONS

Are you guys tired of walking? We already visited all the districts of Venice, heard its stories, and even answered a few questions? Right?

If you'd like now to sit with me, I will tell you all about the holidays and special days we celebrate here in Venice. We have already heard about two holidays from Grandfather Bepi: S. Martino, November 11th (see page 22), and Saint Mark, April 25th (see page 72).

But there are many more...

THE HOLIDAY OF REDENTORE

The holiday of Redentore is one of the most known holidays of Venetians: its origin dates back to the end of the 1500's, when in 1575 Venice was devastated by a the most terrible plague, during which thousands of persons died, one of these was the famous painter Tiziano Vecellio.

The doge urged the citizens to pray and believe that the city would be freed from this plague: soon after the disease was cured. The government then hired the architect Andrea Palladio to design a temple of worship to the Redeemer (Redentore), to build on the island of Giudecca.

The doge decreed that the third Sunday of July would be a day to visit the temple of Redentore and that a bridge of boats be constructed to allow passage of the procession of the doge and patriarch from S. Mark to Giudecca, after which followed the citizens of Venice.

With the passing of time, the holiday began on the eve of Redentore, because the people were afraid not to find a place in the church, so they passed the night in their boats between Bacino San Marco and Giudecca, celebrating in joyfulness: the shores and the boats became decorated with branches, flowers, and balloons of colored paper illuminated inside by candles (which were called the "baloni del Redentòr"). Near midnight the shore became alive with fireworks to greet the Redeemer (Redentore).

This holiday has lasted for centuries, and even today, on the evening of "Redentòr", Venetians gather at the Bacino San Marco in party decorated boats, filled with provisions for dinner.
There, between hundreds of boats and a rowdy crowd, the holiday is celebrated with fireworks, which arrive a half hour before midnight. The next day many cross the bridge of boats from S. Mark to Giudecca continuing this historical pilgrimage to the church of Redentore.

93

HOLIDAY OF THE MADONNA OF THE HEALTH

The holiday of the Madonna della Salute originated at the beginning of 1600: in 1630 a terrible plague exploded in Venice, brought to the Republic by the German soldiers that fought in Lombardy and other cities in the Veneto region. The disease arrived also in Venice and began to spread itself swiftly, until it's suffers were quarantined to the island of S. Clemente.

The lack of hygiene, and the ignorance of the merchants that sold infected garments, helped the plague to spread quickly: in a short period, 50.000 people died; a third of the population of Venice. The Venetians began to pray to the Madonna to free them from this terrible disease against which they were powerless, and gathered themselves every Saturday in prayer in front of the Madonna Nicopeja in S. Mark, together with the patriarch and the doge. The Senate, meanwhile, deliberated and ruled to build a temple in honor of the Madonna, S. Maria of the Health.

The disease miraculously ceased. And as promised, a spectacular church was built, near the Punta della Dogana, facing S. Mark, designed by Baldassarre Longhena, to give thanks to Maria for freeing them from this horrible disease, and it was written that every year the doge must go and visit this temple.

Still today, on November 21, the Venetians pilgrimage to the Madonna of the health by crossing the Grand Canal by a bridge of boats that is built only for this occasion. In the nearby campi, there are stalls that sell sweets, toys and balloons, a grand celebration and a joyous conclusion of this holiday.

HERE A PHOTO OF ME AND LETIZIA THAT JACOPO TOOK OF US DURING THE HOLIDAY OF HEALTH. IT WAS VERY COLD, BUT WE HAD A WONDERFUL TIME VISITING THE STALLS OF SWEETS AND TOYS!

95

CARNIVAL

Venice has always celebrated Carnival since the beginning of its time: there is still evidence of celebrations before Lent in the year 1094, under the doge Vitale Falier.
In 1296, the last day of Carnival festivities, was declared as Fat Tuesday, on this day the celebration and feast becomes official (and began to be celebrated also outside of Venice). Originally, Carnival began the first Sunday of October and the celebrations continued until the days before Lent.

The entire city celebrated during this holiday: in the campi they constructed platforms and stalls for travelling acrobats, jugglers, and musicians. The travelling vendors sold fruit and sweets (frìtole e galani) in the campi. While, in the palaces, the nobles organized balls, and masks were required: Pantalone, Arlecchino, Brighella, Colombina, or simply a black cloak, the tabarro, with the mask of baùta (typical Venetian masks).

Fat Tuesday, which begins the festivities, is also known as the "Flight of the Dove" ("Volo della colombina"): an acrobat slides down a cord from the bell tower of S. Mark until the Doge's Palace, giving tribute to the doge and scattering flowers above the crowd.

With the fall of the Serenissima, in 1797, the celebration of Carnival slowly disappeared.

In 1979, the celebrations were revived after almost 2 centuries. The famous Carnival returned, with shows in the campi and in S. Mark Square, shows for children and concerts of music.

The tradition is reborn in fabulous style, and every year creating a stir of curiosity and masks from all over the world.

97

SECOND SUNDAY OF MAY
VOGALONGA

The Vogalonga is a sport show very common to the Venetian population: this is not a competitive race, but every year about 1000 row boats of all types participate and carry skilled oarsmen, who show there abilities in front of the members of the società remiere, also groups of friends, family, children, grandparents and foreigners of different countries.

The route is about 30 km and runs from Bacino San Marco until the islands of Vignole, Sant' Erasmo, S. Francesco del Deserto. It continues then until Burano, through the Grand Canal of Murano, and returns to Venice passing through the Canale di Cannaregio. The arrival is at Point of the Dogana. The last stroke begins the festivities for all Venetians: the multicolored boats go through the Grand Canal greeting the applauses and encouragement from the Venetians that came to watch along the rive or vaporetto stops.

The Vogalonga was organized for the first time in 1975 by the family Rosa Salva and from a group of friends who love, respect, and admire the rowers and Venetian traditions, and since then, it has been repeated every year and contributes to the protests of citizens against motorboats who produce many wakes from their boats along the Grand Canal.

REGATA STORICA

THIS IS THE BUCINTORO, THE BOAT THAT WAS USED FOR THE DOGE DURING OFFICIAL OCCASIONS: WHEN HE WENT OUT IN SEA WITH THE SHIP DECORATED FOR HOLIDAY OF SENSA, AS GRANDFATHER BEPI TOLD US IN THE STORY OF THE "SPOSALIZIO DEL MARE" (WEDDING TO THE SEA).

100

The historical regata originated in 1315, when it was established that in occasion of the ancient "holiday of Marie", an annual regata would take place (a true and actual competition), after a magnificent procession of bissone, boats of various types that were decorated to represent the noble families, and at the center was the Bucintoro, where the doge sat. The boats in competition were able to have from 8 to 12 rowers, but the long-awaited competition was that of the gondolini with only 2 rowers, in which the winners received the flag of victory.

The route, which still exists today, leaves from S. Elena and runs the entire Grand Canal, where at the end there is a peg placed that signals the boats to turn around and finish at the point called "in volta de Canal" (where the Grand Canal bends towards S. Mark). This takes place before a jury that is situated on the "machina", a large floating platform elaborately decorated.
The jury gave to the first 4 that arrived, the prestigious flags of victory (red, white, green, and dark blue) and a prize in money.

This tradition is still continued today, in the same manner, on the first Sunday of September: first is the historical procession, then the competition. Surrounded by hundreds of boats with Venetians, and spectators, who come out to view the spectacle and cheer on the competitors.

A story of Grandfather Bepi

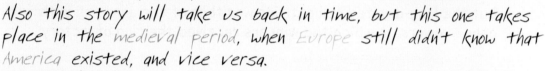

Il Campo dei Mori

Today I will tell you the story of
3 brothers: Rioba, Sandi, and Afani.
Also this story will take us back in time, but this one takes
place in the medieval period, when Europe still didn't know that
America existed, and vice versa.
It was the year 1115, and the 3 brothers, rich spice sellers
who lived in a region of Greece, Morea, left their country due
to political reasons.
The oldest of the 3, Rioba, looked at the map of the world
for an entire night and tried to find a new city to live in.
He wanted to find a modern, independent city that was open
to new ideas and people. But where? Maybe Paris? No, because
there were the French, who were always getting involved in wars.
OK, Roma! ...But the Eastern Emperor always kept an eye on
that city, so it was better to stay far from there...
Sandi returned in that moment from the market. "I met a
man named Alvise", he said, "who spoke to me about a beautiful
city that is in the middle of a lagoon, but trades with the
most important cities of the world: we are sure to find
fortune and fame there. Let's leave as soon as possible
on the ship of Alvise that is getting ready to leave
for Venezia."

102

The 3 brothers were sure of their decision: Venezia.
They opened a spice shop there in Cannaregio, on Fondamenta della Sensa, and here they continued to work in their spice shop and lived for many years in a palace on Rio della Sensa, called "Camel", for the statue that they had in remembrance of their country.
The Venetians called them immediately "I Mori", for the color of their skin and were respected by all inhabitants of the district.
After their death, in memory of Rioba, Sandi, and Afani, 3 marble statues were erected of the 3 brothers dressed in Oriental clothes, with turbans and tunic.
Still today, if you adventure down il Rio della Sensa, in Cannaregio, you will find Campo dei Mori: the 3 statues with the names of the 3 brothers, and if you look on the front of the palace that looks over Rio della Madonna dell'Orto, you will find a camel that is ridden by a man from the far away Eastern country, Morea.

103

Let's play with Jacopo!

Answer the questions: and upon the line going down, you will find the name of a famous Venetian masked man, dressed in red and black, and a small bag upon the belt.

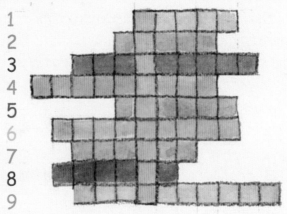

1. Also the painter Tiziano Vecellio died of this...
2. Venetian street...
3. Holiday that precedes Lent...
4. Boat of the doge...
5. The streets of the Gondola's...
6. Sport manifest for row boats...
7. The gift from men on the day of S. Mark...
8. Balloons of colored paper for Redentore...
9. In the comedy of Goldoni, he is the servant of two masters...

104

(solutions are on page 120)

Recipe of Marta
Fritole de Carneval

Ingredients:

600 gr. of flour
25 gr. of yeast
350 cl. of milk
2 eggs
125 gr. of sugar
120 gr. of butter
150 gr. of raisins
50 gr. of pinoli nuts

Mix together the eggs, the sugar, yeast (that must first be melted in a small amount of warm milk), and butter. Add the flour and the rest of the milk, to form a very consistent dough. Add the raisins and the pinoli nuts. Leave to sit for 2 hours. When the dough has risen a bit, fry small spoonfulls of dough in hot oil until they are a nice golden brown color.

Place the fritole on a paper towel (to absorb excess oil) and sprinkle with powdered sugar.

6 - LIVING IN VENICE

Do you want to know what life is like in Venice?
How do we move around if there are no cars?
Where do we put the grocery bags without a trunk?
What do you do when the sirens alert of high water?

There are not large parks or parking garages, there
are not multiplex cinemas but there is an open air cinema.
If you call a taxi, a motorboat arrives, and the bus
is a vaporetto.
How do the children play?
What type of shoes do the mothers wear?

Now I will tell you guys, so come here,
and sit next to me,
between water and land,
between sky and sea.

107

HIGH WATER

Here I am, together with Letizia and with my rain boots: yes, because today there is the high water!
This morning the sirens rang: those which you can find at the top of the bell towers, the same ones from World War II which announced the aerial raids. Now they announce, with certain anticipation, the raid of the tide in the city.
At times they go off at 5 or 6 in the morning: if you have never heard them, I can tell you that they make you shiver!

The alarm goes off when the level of the tide surpasses the 110 cm above sea level, which happens most often during autumn months, and can reach levels of also 130 - 140 cm: then the sleepy citizens must quickly prepare, putting on their rain boots and blocking entrances with steel bulkheads.
The high water has always been a problem: the tide enters from three ports and rises, due to different factors: the phase of the moon, the low pressure, the wind Scirocco that pushes the water from south to north.

To this it is added, in these last years, the meager excavation of the rii that tend to replenish themselves a lot more easily.
As we know, the tide climbs for 6 hours, it stops about half hour and then for other 6 hours goes down, returning at the sea and granting all a chance to breath.

109

EVERYONE IN CAMPO!

Do you want to know where Venetian kids play? In campo, naturally! There is, it is true, some zones with parks, with trees and playgrounds, like Ca' Savorgnan, near Guglie, or the Giardini, in Castello, but the true appointment with rollerblades, bicycles, skates, and ball is in campo: open, spacious, with some trees, and many benches for the mommies. Campo S. Polo, is the largest in the city, during the warm seasons, it is a true place to find children playing. Those who enjoy rollerblading will choose Campo S. Giacomo dell'Orio for its tiled pavement that has just been replaced brand new.

And what about Campo Santa Margherita?
With a fountain to refill bombs of water,
2 delicious ice cream shops, the street towards
the Carmini is a fantastic "track" really slick
What more could you ask for?
Also in Venice, we enjoy the life of open-air,
with a little of fantasy!

HOW DO YOU GET AROUND IN VENICE?

To tell you the truth: Venetians go everywhere by foot.
The historical center can be crossed by foot from one part to
the other, for example from the train station to S. Mark
Square, or Piazzale Roma to Rialto, in about a half hour you can
have a nice walk and come to know the streets that are more
frequented. Naturally it is not advised to wear high heels:
we suggest sneakers!

And, above all, for the tourists who don't know the city very
well, the people in a hurry, the mothers with strollers, and
the small children, there is always the vaporetto: like an
urban bus that runs along the Grand Canal that makes various
stops along the Canal allowing the passengers to get on and
off at different points throughout the city.

The fleet of the ACTV (Azienda del Consorzio Trasporti
Veneziano) is composed of about 150 boats, between vaporetti
and motoscafi, that travel around the canals of Venice and
the outside islands; motonavi, are much larger boats that run
longer courses ending at the shoreline; ferryboat, transports
passengers and cars from the mainland to Lido.

113

IN BOAT

The life of Venice and Venetians is bound to the boat: to move around, to transport goods, to fish, and until some centuries ago, to defend Venice from its enemies.

The Venetian boats are flat in the back in order to move better in the Lagoon where the backs in a lot of points do not leave more than 30-40 cm of water. The most used: the sàndolo, the mascareta, the sciopòn (which is fast and light), the batèla, the caorlina, and boats for transport (which are heavier).

The boats are built in sites called squeri from skilled craftsmen, the axe teachers; to Venice we can see still two squeri still active: S. Trovaso, well-known and characteristic squero for the gondolas and, then nearby, the ancient squero managed from 1800 from the same family, the Tramontin.

THE FORCOLA IS A TRUE AND ACTUAL SCULPTURE IN WOOD WITH 1 OR MORE HOLLOW CUTS TO PLACE THE OAR.

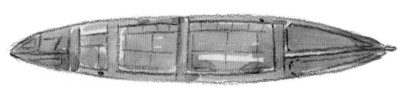

THE **GONDOLA** FROM THE ASYMMETRICAL SHAPE IS LONG 10.85 M AND WIDE 1.40 M WEIGHS ABOUT 400 KG.

THE GONDOLA

The boat most famous, refined and elegant, and is almost
the symbol of the city, is the gondola.
What we see today it is the result of a slow three
formation that happened over the centuries,
in the shape, and dimensions: we find the
name "gondolam" for the first time in 1094,
in a decree of the doge. The gondola is
a very complex construction: alone the
hull is composed of 280 pieces in 7 different
woods. Its shape is asymmetrical: the stern,
in fact lifts itself from the water like a
jerking structure, it is aestheticly attractive,
in order to carry the weight of the gondolier.
The iron post at the bow has 6 teeth,
symbol of the 6 districts.

ANIMALS OF THE CITY

THE **SEAGULLS** COLOR THE VENETIAN SKYS WITH THEIR WEIGHTLESS FLIGHTS, AND WITH THEIR TYPICAL CALL, THAT SEEMS A LAUGH. THEY FOLLOW BEHIND SOME OF THE MOTONAVI, GATHERING THEMSELVES IN THE SUNSET IN LARGE GROUPS ABOVE THE **GRAND CANAL**; IN VENICE THEY ARE CALLED "COCAI"..

THE **PIGEONS** ARE VERY NUMEROUS IN VENICE. THEY MAKE THEIR NESTS UNDER THE MOULDINGS OF CHURCHES AND ON THE UNDISTURBED ROOFTOPS OF THE PALACES. THEY ARE ALWAYS SERACHING, AND READY TO LAND, FOR A SINGLE CRUMB OF BREAD. THEY ARE FOUND EVERYWHERE, BUT ABOVE ALL, IN PIAZZA SAN MARCO, WHERE THEY RECEIVE SEEDS AND CORN FROM THE **TOURISTS**.

THERE IS NOT AN ANGLE OF VENICE IN WHICH THERE IS NOT A DISTINGUISHED CAT: LYING IN THE SUN, ABOVE A WINDOW, ALONG THE CANALS WAITING FOR A CRAB. EVEN IF FREE AND WITHOUT AN OWNER, THE CATS ARE LOVED IN THE CITY: MORE CATS, LESS MICE!

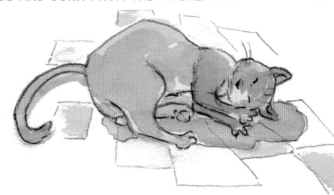

...AND FROM THE SEA

FISHING HAS REMAINED ONE OF THE PRINCIPAL ATTIVITIES OF VENETIANS, EVEN IF IT IS MOSTLY DEDICATED AS A MAJOR SOURCE OF COMMERCE. THE CITIZENS OF THE SERENISSIMA REPUBLIC, IN ORDER TO PRESERVE MARINE LIFE, ENFORCED A LIMIT TO THE NUMBER OF FISH CAUGHT AND SOLD IN THE MARKET. A MARBLE PLAQUE WITH A LIST OF THESE LIMITED NUMBERS IS STILL VISIBLE IN THE FISHMARKET OF CAMPO SANTA MARGHERITA (SEE PAGE 40).

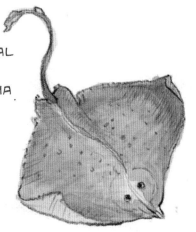

RAZZA

ORATA

SOME TYPICAL VENETIAN FISH DISHES:
THE "MOECHE", WHICH ARE SOFT CRABS THAT ARE FISHED DURING THEIR MOULTING PERIOD;
THE "BISATO IN TOCIO", WHICH IS AN EEL STEW;
THE "SEPE (CUTTLEFISHES) IN NERO", WITH WHICH YOU CAN MAKE EXCELLENT RISOTTO.

BISATO (ANGUILLA)

117

A story of Grandfather Bepi

The lace of Burano

This last story that I will tell you brings us to the island of Burano, many years ago.

Here on this island of a "1.000 colors" in the middle of the Lagoon, between Mazzorbo and Torcello, the women have sat for centuries with thread and needle, giving life to the most beautiful lace; sewn with great artistry, beautiful style, and amazing craft and skill. But how was this tradition of Burano lace begun?

Once upon a time, many many years ago, a young fisherman from Burano named Zuane, was in love with Costanza, the most beautiful girl on the island. She had eyes as green and transparent as the lagoon, eyes that you dreamt of in day and night.

They saw each other as much as possible, but Zuane was always afraid that someone else would steal away the beautiful Costanza. So, he thought and thought, and he decided that he wanted to give her the most beautiful gift, something that would truely show his great love for her. He searched for days in his "sandolo" throughout the Lagoon, with bucket and pail, until he finally found a beautiful and very rare sea plant, that no one has ever seen two alike.

118

That night, Costanza brought this rare lagoon flower back to her house, and she placed it with care above a silk hankerchief in her room: "This air and this light is sure to destroy it", she thought, "I have to find a way to conserve it forever".
The next day, she put herself to work: and with thread and needle, patiently and with great love, she copied every leaf, every stem, and every petal of that beautiful sea plant.

She worked for three days and three nights, uninterrupted. The little plant was already dried up, but between the hands of Costanza it was reblossomed forever, with a thread of love, in a splendid lace.

119

Let's play with Jacopo!

In the blank space below draw a picture
of your cat (or your favorite animal).
If you need a starting point, I put here
a picture of Lula licking her paw.
Good work!

Oh, and by the way, here are the solutions
to the previous games. Were you able to
answer them all? Good!

Page 24 - the candy
Page 88 - 1. Grado, Torcello, Malamocco
         2. Paoluccio Anafesto
         3. Alexandria of Egypt
         4. the Fouth Crusades, il doge Enrico Dandolo
Page 104- Pantalone (Peste, Calle, Carnevale, Bucintoro,
          Canali, Vogalonga, Boccolo, Baloni, Arlecchino)

The recipe of Marta
i buranelli

Ingredients:

500 gr. flour
3 eggs
200 gr. sugar
150 gr. butter
1 peeled lemon skin
baking powder
a pinch of salt

Mix together all the ingredients until you have obtained a soft dough, but solid. Taking pieces of dough, make long rolls that you can shape into the form of a "S" or a ring.

Put the cookies on a baking tray covered with a sheet of baking paper and bake at 180° for about 15-20 minutes.
Take them out of the oven while they are still soft, and when they cool they will become more dry.

121

Well kids, unfortunatly our trip is over!
Did you have fun? We did very much!

Here there are empty pages left for
you to write notes, drawings, thoughts,
or poetry.
Don't forget to always look around:
in ever corner of Venice there are
always treasures to discover!

We hope to see you again in an exciting
walk through Venice, we live here,
over that bridge!

Goodbye to all of you!

Marta, Jacopo, Letizia... and Lula!

123

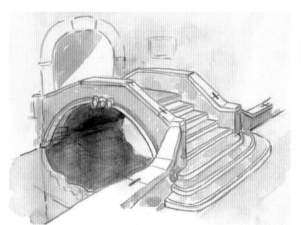

MY NOTES...

MY NOTES....

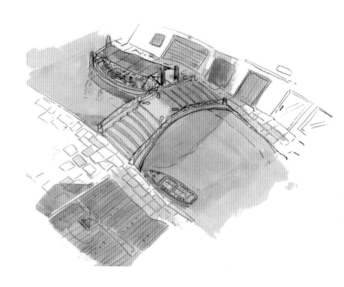

MY NOTES....

MY NOTES....

MY NOTES....

SUMMARY

1 - HOW IS VENICE MADE?

2- THE DISTRICTS

3- SAINT MARK

4- VENICE AND ITS STORY

5- HOLIDAYS AND TRADITIONS

6- LIVING IN VENICE

Maria Gianola was born in Venice, where she still
works and lives.
In her childhood she started to draw with passion,
then she studies History of Art, Drawing and
Painting. Recently she illustreted books for
children with several editors.
Also she had three children (very interested in
reading books). This work is dedicated to them.